A GUIDE TO CONVERSATIONAL AI: CHATGPT FOR HIGHER EDUCATION AND PROFESSIONAL DEVELOPMENT

AKANKSH REDDY MUDDAM

Made with ♥ on the Notion Press Platform
www.notionpress.com

To the Loving Memory of my Grandmother, Mrs Chakraveni.

Grandma, you are the cause of everything! Without my grandma's perseverance and strong resolve, I would not be here today.

Contents

Acknowledgements

This text was created in part using OpenAI's large-scale language-generation model GPT-3. The author, who is ultimately responsible for this publication's content, reviewed, edited, and amended the wording after it had been generated as a draught.

The following people and organisations are also appreciated:

The ChatGPT model was created and maintained by the OpenAI team, who also made it accessible to the research community.

Family and friends who supported and inspired you while you were writing.

My work has been influenced by scholars, practitioners, and organisations who have made contributions to the field of AI safety, ethics, and responsible use.

The ChatGPT model was fine-tuned for the studies detailed in this paper using the Hugging Face's transformers library.

Contents

Preface

I was interested to learn more about ChatGPT as a student and IT enthusiast. I made the decision to try it out for myself, and the realistic conversational agent, the extensive capabilities, and the captivating user design really blew me away. I started experimenting with sending emails using ChatGPT. To my astonishment, I managed to reach inbox zero for the first time in just a few short weeks.

As I persisted in fiddling with ChatGPT, an idea for a guide started to form in my head. I was interested in learning more about how this formidable technology might affect both higher education and society at large. At the University of Rhode Island College of Business, I opened up talks with some of my colleagues. I was impressed by their openness and enthusiasm about the potential applications of generative AI in teaching and learning.

I was persuaded that ChatGPT may have a significant impact on how we teach and learn as I dove farther down the rabbit hole of speculating about its potential. I created "A Guide to Conversational AI: ChatGPT for Higher Education and Professional Development" because I wanted to share my insights with others.

Through my investigation and testing, I have come to realise that ChatGPT has the ability to profoundly alter the way we see education and learning in addition to being an effective tool for automating repetitive chores and streamlining communication. I think that by making ChatGPT easier to use and comprehend, students, teachers, and professionals may take use of this successful tool to increase productivity, effectiveness, and societal impact.

The active community of experimenters and innovators that are already finding and sharing new methods to use ChatGPT in my work struck me as I started to write this guide. I was motivated by these people's inventiveness and innovation, and I hope my guide will be helpful to anyone interested in learning more about the potential of this cutting-edge technology. I am eager to share my experience, guide others as they use ChatGPT at work, and explore its potential.

An intellectual sparring partner who can engage with you in thought-provoking conversations, a dedicated research assistant who can quickly access information and conversely fulfil your requests, and an administrative assistant who can help you draught reports and business copy are all things that ChatGPT can be. You may have different viewpoints and factors to take into account while integrating ChatGPT into your teaching, learning, and professional practice as a student, educator, or professional. While some may view ChatGPT as a useful tool to increase productivity and efficiency, others might be concerned about how adopting such cutting-edge technology might affect human job duties and ethical issues.We must take into account all viewpoints and approach the integration of ChatGPT with care and consideration. This guide seeks to offer direction and insights for individuals who want to use ChatGPT's capabilities in their work efficiently while also addressing ethical issues.

This guide, which was created with assistance from ChatGPT during the project's prewriting, writing, and revision phases, is an investigation of ChatGPT for higher education. I read this material over and updated it. I used Grammarly's plagiarism detection tool to confirm that this work is entirely original, and I accept full responsibility for its content. Writing this manual taught me how to write with ChatGPT, what makes it perform well, and what makes it produce less helpful content. The goals and information in this manual are specifically designed for academics who are learning about and extending their use of ChatGPT.

This manual is not intended to be the last or most comprehensive guide to ChatGPT for higher education. Please think of this manual as a starting point rather than a complete manual for all applications of ChatGPT.
In order to raise awareness of what is possible as AI-powered chatbot technology alters university teaching and learning, let this serve as an example of the potential of the most recent generation of chatbot technology. It is intended to assist you in comprehending the potential advantages and disadvantages of utilising ChatGPT in higher education and to provide you with the information and resources you need to make an informed choice about its application to your own teaching, learning, and other activities.

In this manual, you will learn:

1. How ChatGPT can improve writing, communication, and learning for university students, teachers, and professionals

2. How to provide compelling cues so that ChatGPT can assist
3. Guidelines for utilising ChatGPT in an ethical and responsible manner

This manual can be an invaluable tool for a variety of people and organisations wishing to include ChatGPT in their instruction, learning, and professional practice. It serves as an introduction to ChatGPT for higher education, outlining its features and prospective applications. It can also serve as a convenient desk reference for adding to your ChatGPT toolset and discovering more sophisticated features and methods. It can also be given as reading for a class or group that is researching or using ChatGPT in their particular field. It is my aim that through utilising the potential of ChatGPT, readers would be motivated to find fresh perspectives and techniques to improve their teaching, learning, and professional practice.

The structure of this manual is as follows. In Chapter 1, the reader is introduced to ChatGPT in the context of higher education, and in Chapter 2, the reader is given the facts and common myths about ChatGPT. A step-by-step introduction is provided in Chapter 3 to help you get started, and Chapter 4 offers practise for more proficient ChatGPT prompting while reinforcing key ideas. More writing and conversation prompts are provided in Chapters 5 and 6, and Chapter 7 looks at how professionals may use ChatGPT for specialised training, instruction, and treatment. The discussion of ethics and responsible ChatGPT use for higher education finish Chapter 8.

You will learn new ways that ChatGPT may revolutionise a variety of routine tasks associated with teaching, learning, and professional life as we explore the frontier of generative AI for higher education with this book. This book will introduce you to the fascinating potential of this ground-breaking technology, and it is my hope that it will motivate you to consider how ChatGPT may improve your own instruction, learning, and professional practise.

CHAPTER ONE

CHATGPT IN HIGHER EDUCATION

1.1 Introduction: What exactly is ChatGPT?

The advanced language model ChatGPT (Generative Pre-trained Transformer), created by OpenAI, employs artificial intelligence to produce text that resembles human writing. The public release of ChatCPT on November 30, 2022, was a substantial advancement in language model technology. It opened up new opportunities for language models and has increased their capacity to carry out a variety of tasks. It demonstrated remarkable progress in the ability to understand and produce human-like writing.

It is beneficial for a variety of activities thanks to its capacity for naturalistic understanding and response to linguistic input, particularly in the context of higher education. It can be taught to carry out particular duties, such as finishing a conversation you've started or responding to inquiries. You can utilise ChatGPT to aid you with your writing by using it as your research assistant, receiving personalised feedback, and enhancing your interpersonal communication.

"How can professionals, educators, and college students use ChatGPT?"

All you need is a free OpenAI account to ask questions like this, and ChatGPT will respond. Visit the ChatGPT chat interface at http://www.openai.com to register right away if you haven't already. In Chapter 3, we'll go into greater detail about the beginning. Entering the aforementioned prompt in the browser-based ChatGPT interface triggers the LLM to produce an especially designed message, such as:

College students can use ChatGPT for several activities, including research and writing projects, text summaries and paraphrases, and even the creation of creative writing prompts. Teachers can utilise ChatGPT to develop interactive tests, lesson plans, and teaching resources. Professionals can utilise ChatGPT for things like summarising a lot of data, preparing reports, and making presentations. Additionally, by automatically creating answers to frequent queries, ChatGPT can be utilised for customer care and assistance.

The user may now type content or copy and paste it. In a chat, the user and ChatGPT alternate text entries in this fashion. ChatGPT is coachable and receptive to follow-up inquiries or more guidance. Currently, ChatGPT and other language models are used in higher education in several contexts, including teaching and learning, research, and institutional development.

As you begin utilising ChatGPT, you can do so properly and fully utilise its features. By thoughtfully incorporating ChatGPT into your business, you can create new chances for innovation, efficiency, and creativity. The possibilities and potential of ChatGPT are extremely exciting.

1.2 Present-day Language Model Applications in Higher Education

You may be asking how else ChatGPT can be applied to higher education as students, teachers, and professionals. The approach has the power to alter how we educate people. It has a wide range of uses, including writing and brainstorming exercises, business communications, and personalised learning.

Operations management is a crucial topic in MBA schools, thus Christian Terwiesch, a Wharton professor at the University of Pennsylvania, tested the chatbot's proficiency in this area. He discovered that the chatbot scored between a B and a B- on the test, and he came to the conclusion that this had significant ramifications for business school instruction, emphasising the need to examine testing procedures, curriculum development, and instruction.

"Chat GPT3 would have scored between a B and a B- on the test. In his white paper "Would Chat GPT3 Get an MBA from Wharton?," Terwiesch stated that this has significant ramifications for the business school curriculum.

Professor Jerry Davis of the Ross School of Business at the University of Michigan declared, "I'm one of the alarmists." This is a challenge for our entire educational industry, and it will only get harder. It's time to completely reassess everything."

"We are having serious discussions and a working group is looking at the implications of ChatGPT and other similar tools that we know our resourceful and inventive students are using, and we will be formulating policies around that soon," said Francisco Veloso, dean of Imperial College Business School in London.

"I was in awe of the writing's beauty—its clarity, word choice, and organisation. Terwiesch commented, "It was incredibly fantastic, but the arithmetic is so terrible. Language and intuition are accurate, yet even high school math was largely incorrect. 3

Using ChatGPT to assist with brainstorming and writing is one of its most important uses in higher education. The model can be taught to comprehend the precise formatting and style requirements of a task or paper and can offer suggestions and adjustments to enhance the writing's coherence and clarity. Students that struggle with writing or non-native speakers can benefit the most from this. For instance, a student can use ChatGPT to come up with essay topic ideas and receive editorial input.

Professional communication is another important ChatGPT use in higher education. ChatGPT can be used to create professional emails, reports, and other documents. It can also be used to rehearse real-world situations by simulating them. For instance, a professional can create an email for a customer using ChatGPT and receive comments on the email's tone and style. Individualized learning is yet another application of ChatGPT in higher education. Based on the student's learning preferences and development, the model can produce exercises and quizzes, offer feedback, and be used to create individualised learning programmes and instructional materials. For instance, a student can create flashcards using ChatGPT that are specific to their learning requirements.

ChatGPT has a lot of potentials, but it also has certain drawbacks. Because a model can only be as good as the data it is trained on, it might not be able to comprehend or react to certain types of input or might give biased or erroneous results. Additionally, because it creates text based on patterns it has identified in the training data, it occasionally produces grammatically incorrect or illogical language. While ChatGPT can be a helpful tool for brainstorming and writing assistance, professional communications, and individualised learning, it is vital to remember that it must be used responsibly and with an understanding of its possibilities and limitations.

Detailed examples of language model usage in higher education are provided below, along with sample ChatGPT prompts.

1. Computerized essay grading

Language models can be taught to comprehend and evaluate student essays, giving teachers a quick and precise approach to evaluating their students' writing.

"Would you please grade this student's essay on the effect of technology on education?"

2. Individualized instruction

Language models can be used to give pupils individualised feedback and direction as they solve problems or finish assignments.

"Can you provide this student individual feedback and direction on this math problem?"

3. Providing research

Researchers can utilise language models to help them find pertinent material, come up with hypotheses, and write articles.

'Artificial Intelligence in Higher Education' is a topic I'm looking for relevant literature on.

4. In-class support

Teachers can get assistance from language models when making lesson plans, presentations, and other types of resources.

Can you assist me in developing a lesson plan on "The History of AI"?

5. Language interpretation

To translate educational resources and improve their accessibility for staff and students who speak different languages, language models might be employed.

The educational material needs to be translated from English to Spanish.

6. Development of writing, research, and communication skills

Students that use language models in their writing, research, and communication can get better results.

Can you give this student feedback on their research paper on "Chatbot technology in education" to help them become better writers?

7. Professors can also use ChatGPT to create their syllabi, tests, and exams.

For my AI class, can you assist me in creating a quiz on the subject of "Natural Language Processing"?

8. Language models can also be used to create summaries, reports, and other materials linked to the study.

Can you assist me in summarising this academic paper on "AI in education"?

9. Chatbot and email support

ChatGPT can be used to build chatbots, which are automated email replies that can help faculty, staff, and students with typical inquiries. Administrators may have more time to devote to more difficult responsibilities as a result.

"Can you assist me in developing an automated email answer for typical student queries?"

10. Organizing events and meetings

By suggesting time slots, generating agendas, and even producing meeting minutes, ChatGPT can be used to help schedule meetings and activities.

"Can you assist set up a meeting and provide an agenda for next week?"

11. Support for campus tours

The campus can be virtually toured via ChatGPT, giving potential students and their families a fun and interactive opportunity to learn more about the school.

Can you assist me in giving potential students a virtual tour of the university?

12. Assistance with policies and procedures

By offering language suggestions, giving examples, and even highlighting possible issue areas, educators can use ChatGPT to help develop language for changing university rules and procedures.

"Can you assist me by offering language suggestions and highlighting potential problem areas for updating the university's policy on "Use of AI in the classroom"?"

13. Producing reports

Reports on enrollment, graduation rates, finances, and other aspects of university operations can be produced by administrators using ChatGPT.

"Could you produce a report on student enrollment figures for the most recent semester?"

These are some instances of how university administrators in higher education can use ChatGPT. Numerous uses are possible because of this technology's adaptability, and more use cases will likely be created as it develops.

1.3 ChatGPT in Higher Education: Issues and Limitations

While ChatGPT and other language models have the potential to fundamentally change how we teach, learn, and carry out research in higher education, several difficulties and restrictions must be taken into account while using these tools.

The number of characters that can be entered into the console is capped at 1,000, and the rate at which messages are sent is throttled.

The potential for ChatGPT and other language models to reinforce societal prejudices and discrimination is one of the primary issues. Large amounts of data are used to train these models, and if the data is skewed, the model's output will reflect that bias. This might be a drawback when applying them to processes that demand impartiality and fairness, like hiring or grading.

The possibility that ChatGPT and other language models will be applied in ways that are inconsistent with our values and beliefs presents another difficulty. ChatGPT might be used, for instance, to impose rules on people's behaviour and thoughts or to reinforce prejudices already present in society.

The possibility for ChatGPT and other language models to be misused in negative ways is a third problem. They might be applied to strengthen social problems already present, such as discrimination, or they might be applied to establish a surveillance state.

The inability to comprehend human emotions, motivations and moral reasoning is another drawback. ChatGPT and other language models are unable to comprehend moral reasoning, emotions, or intentions in people. This can be a drawback when applying them to jobs that demand empathy, like counselling or tutoring.

The difficulty of guaranteeing the output quality of the language models is another one. Language models are not perfect; they can produce mistakes or give incorrect answers. When used for jobs requiring high degrees of accuracy, such as evaluating essays or making medical diagnoses, this can be a drawback.

When adopting language models in higher education, such as ChatGPT, be mindful of these difficulties and restrictions. We can ensure that language models are utilised responsibly and ethically and that they have the greatest influence on teaching, learning, and research in higher education by being aware of these difficulties and adopting measures to address them.

1.4 Language Model Comparison in Higher Education

One of the many well-liked language models now being employed in higher education is ChatGPT. The BERT, GPT-2, and RoBERTa language models are among the more well-known ones. Even though each of these models has the potential to influence how we teach, learn, and carry out research in higher education, there are some significant distinctions between them in terms of their potential and constraints.

OpenAI created ChatGPT, a sophisticated language model that was trained on a wide variety of internet material. This enables it to produce writing that appears human and responds to inquiries. ChatGPT excels in comprehending context and producing content that is well-organized and cohesive.

BERT: Designed by Google, BERT is a model based on transformers that have been trained on a variety of internet text. BERT is exceptional in deciphering the meaning of the text and is particularly skilled at jobs like text production, question answering, and natural language understanding. BERT struggles to comprehend the context and produce content that is well-formed and coherent.

GPT-2 is a large-scale language model that was created by OpenAI and trained on a wide variety of internet literature. GPT-2 has a wide range of uses, including text generation, question answering, and natural language understanding. It is renowned for its capacity to produce writing that is human-like. GPT-2 has, however, drawn flak for being difficult to read.

RoBERTa is a transformer-based model that was created by Facebook and trained on a variety of internet materials. RoBERTa does exceptionally well at tasks like natural language understanding, question resolution, and text generation. It also excels at grasping the meaning of the text. RoBERTa is an enhanced variant of BERT that is more efficient than BERT in specific tasks, although it uses a lot more computer power.

In conclusion, sophisticated language models such as ChatGPT, BERT, GPT-2, and RoBERTa have the potential to transform how we teach, learn, and carry out research in higher education. Every model has advantages and disadvantages, and the optimal option will depend on the application and use case at hand. Although ChatGPT has been demonstrated to reinforce bias found in the data it was trained on, it is notable for producing writing that appears human-like and responding to questions. BERT, on the other hand, is extremely adept at comprehending natural language, responding to questions, and producing text. However, it struggles to comprehend the context and produce writing that is cohesive and well-formed.

Although GPT-2 is renowned for its capacity to produce language that resembles that of a human, it has come under fire for lacking interpretability and having the tendency to reinforce bias in its training data. Although RoBERTa is an enhanced version of BERT that performs better than BERT at grasping the meaning of the text, it uses a lot more processing power.

Artificial intelligence is a discipline that is constantly developing thanks to new research and innovations in fields like machine learning, natural language processing, computer vision, and others. The following are some of the most recent AI studies:

1. Adversarial machine learning

The goal of this research is to provide techniques for safeguarding AI systems against harmful assaults, such as building "adversarial instances" that can deceive an AI model.

2. Explainable AI

As opposed to being mysterious "black boxes," there is rising interest in creating AI systems that can explain their conclusions in plain, understandable language.

3. Reinforcement learning

Instead of using supervised learning, this method of machine learning includes training AI models through trial and error.

4. Generative AI

Based on what they have learnt from a dataset, these kinds of AI models are capable of producing new data, such as images or text.

5. Conversational AI and Chatbots

This branch of AI entails developing tools like ChatGPT that can comprehend and react to input in natural language.

1.5 ChatGPT and Professional Growth

University students, teachers, and professionals can use ChatGPT as a tool to help them become aware of the potential that AI has to change many facets of their area.

For students, AI can offer individualised criticism and direction while also assisting in the development of communication and writing abilities. Along with practical knowledge of the crucial AI components of language production and natural language processing.

In addition to helping teachers assess student work and create lesson plans, presentations, and other materials, AI may also help teachers create their syllabuses, quizzes, and exams. Additionally, it can assist teachers in assessing students' development and giving them tailored comments.

Professionals may increase their productivity by using AI to aid with tasks like meeting scheduling, report writing, and presentation creation. Giving them insights and forecasts, can assist them in making better decisions and even improve their ability to interact with coworkers and clients.

In conclusion, AI may benefit students, teachers, and professionals greatly by giving them more productive and efficient ways to work, learn, and communicate. They seek to prepare AI to gain from these advantages and maintain their competitiveness in the quick-paced environment of today.

Students, teachers, and professionals can gain a greater grasp of AI principles and methods through the use of ChatGPT, including the value of data and the function of neural networks in language generation. They will be more equipped to deal with AI in a professional setting if they have a greater understanding of how AI systems operate.

Chapter Overview

The usage of ChatGPT, a sizable language model created by OpenAI, in higher education is covered in Chapter 1. The chapter describes how ChatGPT analyses enormous amounts of text data and produces text responses that resemble those of human beings in response to commands. The chapter makes note of ChatGPT's numerous uses, such as writing aid, language acquisition, and research, which are altering how students study and teachers teach in higher education. The chapter also emphasises ChatGPT's shortcomings, such as the possibility of providing biased or incorrect results and being only as good as the data it is trained on. Additionally, the chapter gives instances of how language models are currently being used in higher education, including automated essay grading, individualised tutoring, and language translation.

CHAPTER TWO

CHATGPT MYTHS AND FACTS

The powers and restrictions of this potent language model are introduced in Chapter 2, "Myths and Facts about ChatGPT." This chapter will examine popular myths regarding ChatGPT, such as the idea that using it properly constitutes plagiarism and the idea that it can take the place of actual teachers. Additionally, it will give important information about ChatGPT, such as how it may be used as a support tool in higher education and how it keeps getting better over time. This chapter will also look into ChatGPT's effects on the AI-enabled workforce and emphasise the value of ethical technology use. The chapter will also discuss ChatGPT's usability by non-technical users. By debunking some common misconceptions about ChatGPT, readers will be better prepared to choose whether or not to use it in particular applications.

2.1 Five ChatGPT Myths

2.1.1 Myth: Using ChatGPT properly disclosed constitutes plagiarism

It is a fallacy that admitting to using GPT-3 would constitute plagiarism. The practice of presenting someone else's ideas as your own without giving them due credit is known as plagiarism. However, you must explicitly mention that you used the GPT-3 model and provide credit to the appropriate source when using it. In addition to being moral, doing this supports the integrity of your work. You must follow the ChatGPT usage policy as well as any classroom management guidelines set forth by your instructor, the academic integrity requirements of your university, and any applicable laws. It is essential to properly credit or acknowledge ChatGPT to uphold the integrity of your work and follow ethical standards.

2.1.2 Myth: ChatGPT is only practical for straightforward jobs

It's a prevalent misperception that ChatGPT and other language models are only effective for straightforward jobs. This is not the case, though. Beyond simple tasks, ChatGPT and other language models have a wide range of features and possible uses.

Advanced algorithms that can comprehend and produce natural language are the foundation of ChatGPT and other language models. This makes them helpful for a variety of jobs, including

Play the role of a lawyer and make a case for why a defendant in a criminal trial should be found not guilty.

Take on the role of a financial expert and offer a prediction for the stock market in the upcoming quarter.

Play the role of a doctor and describe the available therapies to a patient with a certain illness.

Play the historian and offer a cause-and-effect analysis of a certain historical event.

Play the politician and deliver a speech in support of a particular political subject.

Take on the role of a detective and provide information to solve a made-up crime.

Play the role of a teacher and develop a lesson plan for a certain mathematical subject.

A longer set of customised "act as a" prompts compiled from a GitHub repository specifically for ChatGPT prompts may be found in the Appendix.

Some "act as a" prompts are more complicated and continue to be beyond ChatGPT's existing capabilities as ChatGPT increases its features. Examples of such questions are:

Become a medical professional and determine a patient's condition from their symptoms

Take on the role of a legal professional and offer a thorough analysis of a particular court case

Play the role of a financial expert by offering a thorough evaluation of a company's financial statements.

In conclusion, ChatGPT and other language models are effective resources that may be applied to a variety of tasks and objectives in a variety of academic and professional sectors. These tools can be used in several ways to help higher education and beyond, as opposed to being restricted to straightforward tasks.

2.1.3 Myth: ChatGPT can take the role of real instructors and professors.

One common misunderstanding regarding ChatGPT and other language models is that they may take the place of real professors and teachers. This is untrue, though. Even while ChatGPT and other language models are cutting-edge tools that can support teaching and learning, they cannot take the place of human educators' distinctive talents and skills.

The foundation of ChatGPT and other language models are sophisticated algorithms that have been trained on a sizable amount of data. These algorithms are capable of comprehending and producing genuine language, but they are unable to comprehend the specifics and nuances of a certain subject or sector. Additionally, they are unable to provide individualised learning experiences for pupils or give them feedback and direction.

Consider a student in a mathematics class who is having trouble understanding a challenging idea, for instance. A human teacher would be better able to comprehend the student's particular challenges and offer appropriate comments and direction to aid in the student's comprehension of the idea. Contrarily, while ChatGPT can explain a subject, it is unable to comprehend the student's unique challenges and offers customised comments.

Furthermore, ChatGPT and other language models are unable to comprehend students' emotional and psychological requirements or to offer the same level of social and emotional support that real teachers and professors can. Human teachers are capable of comprehending their pupils' emotional and psychological requirements and providing the assistance required for students to achieve. This is demonstrated by their capacity to foster a supportive and welcoming learning atmosphere in the classroom, which is crucial for retaining and motivating students.

In conclusion, ChatGPT and other language models can be helpful teaching and learning aids, but they cannot take the place of real professors and teachers. They are not able to take the place of human educators' distinctive skills and abilities, but they can help them in their work by offering more resources and support.

Colleges and universities must be aware of the limitations of these tools and use them to support human educators rather than replace them. This can entail utilising them in addition to conventional teaching strategies or as a way to give pupils extra support outside of the classroom. Colleges and universities can use ChatGPT and other language models in this way to gain the advantages of these tools while preserving the human connection necessary for successful teaching and learning.

2.1.4 Myth: ChatGPT is unreliable and biased

The possibility of bias and unreliability in ChatGPT and other language models is a worry. This is a legitimate worry because these models are trained using a tonne of data, and if the data is biased, the model will also be skewed. The quality of the data used to train the model, the nature of the task it is used for, and how it is employed can all have an impact on how well it performs.

If the prompts or queries are not carefully written, ChatGPT and other language models may stray from the intended course. The model may produce biased or irrelevant results, for instance, if the prompts use biased language or are not explicit enough.

It's crucial to pay attention to how the prompts are worded to get more pertinent responses. Here are some illustrations of how to thoughtfully word prompts:

1. Use language that is clear and precise.

Ask "What are some philosophical perspectives on the purpose of life?" as opposed to "What is the meaning of life?"

2. Steer clear of racist words

Ask "What are some common career alternatives for people regardless of their gender" instead of "What are the best careers for women?"

3. Present background

Asking "What city is the French National Assembly located in?" is a better question than "What is the capital of France?"

In Chapter 4, we go through what makes a prompt more pertinent. Be precise: Asking "What are some evidence-based tactics for managing stress in the workplace?" is a better question than "What are the best ways to minimise stress?" It is feasible to get ChatGPT and other language models to deliver more pertinent and accurate responses by paying attention to how the prompts are framed.

2.1.5 Myth: ChatGPT cannot be used by non-technical individuals.

It's a common misperception that persons with technical expertise can only use ChatGPT and other language paradigms. This is not accurate, though. The use of user-friendly interfaces, as well as the provision of clear and understandable documentation and tutorials, can make these products accessible to non-technical users.

Through a browser interface, non-technical users can engage with the model without the need for any specialised training or technical knowledge. This is one method that non-technical users can use ChatGPT. For instance, even if a non-technical individual lacks a solid background in computer science or data science and works in an area like finance or healthcare, they can still utilise ChatGPT to analyse data, provide reports, or build chatbots for customer service. They don't need any specialised training to input data, set parameters, and receive output using the browser interface.

Another illustration of how non-technical people might utilise ChatGPT is to validate the model's output without the requirement for technical expertise. For instance, even if a non-technical person lacks machine learning expertise and works in a profession like media or research, they can still utilise ChatGPT to produce summaries or insights from big data sets. The output of the model can then be cross-checked with data from other sources or tested using other tools to ensure its accuracy.

In conclusion, even though ChatGPT and other language models can be complicated, non-technical individuals can still use these technologies.

2.2 Five ChatGPT-Related Facts

2.2.1 Fact: ChatGPT is a valuable resource for higher education

Higher education can greatly benefit from ChatGPT and other language paradigms. These resources can be used for many purposes, such as assisting with writing, learning a new language, conducting research, and managing projects.

Writing support is one of the most obvious ways that ChatGPT might be beneficial in higher education. Students and teachers can save time and improve the quality of their writing by using the model to generate text, summaries, and outlines. The model can also be used to check for grammatical and stylistic faults, which can enhance the readability and clarity of written material.

Language learning is yet another application of ChatGPT in higher education. The concept can be used to produce translations, summaries tailored to different languages, and comprehension activities that can aid both students and teachers in developing their language proficiency.

ChatGPT can help researchers quickly and easily detect patterns and insights that would be challenging to uncover manually by analysing data and summarising enormous volumes of data. The model can also be used to produce research proposals, literature reviews, and other documents connected to the research.

2.2.2 Fact: ChatGPT is constantly getting better

Natural language interpretation, machine learning, and data processing are just a few of the areas where ChatGPT and other language models are constantly getting better.

The ability of ChatGPT to grasp natural language is one of its main areas of improvement. The model is getting trained on a larger and more varied set of data, which is assisting it to comprehend and react to a wide range of inputs and inquiries better. The model's capacity to comprehend and produce content is being enhanced further by the usage of fresh methodologies including transfer learning and fine-tuning.

Machine learning is another area where ChatGPT is developing. The model is being trained on more sophisticated architectures, such as transformer models, which is assisting in enhancing its accuracy and performance. To enhance the model's capacity for text translation and comprehension, new methodologies including neural machine translation and question answering are also being applied.

Finally, ChatGPT is getting better at processing data. The model is being trained on a wider range of datasets and can handle data from more languages. Additionally, the model is being tuned to operate on more potent technology, enabling faster and more effective data processing.

In conclusion, ChatGPT and other language models are constantly developing in fields like data processing, machine learning, and natural language understanding. The model is becoming more precise, effective, and able to handle a larger range of inputs and queries thanks to these developments. Thus, ChatGPT and other language models will be able to produce results that are more accurate and valuable.

2.2.3 Fact: ChatGPT works best as a support tool.

Although ChatGPT and other language models are extremely effective tools, they shouldn't be used in place of real instructors and professors. Instead, it is ideal to use these technologies as supplementary tools to improve teaching, learning, and research.

The inability of ChatGPT and other language models to comprehend and interpret context and nuance in the same manner that people can is one of the key reasons why they are best employed as support tools. Although language models are capable of producing writing that resembles that of a human, they fall short of a human instructor or professor in terms of comprehension and empathy. Therefore, keep in mind that human education should still be employed in addition to ChatGPT and other language models, not instead of it.

However, ChatGPT and other language models have a lot of great applications. For instance, ChatGPT can be used to produce individualised feedback on student assignments and tests, to aid with research by generating hypotheses or analysing vast volumes of data, and to assist with administrative duties like arranging appointments or responding to commonly asked inquiries.

Additionally, ChatGPT and other language models can improve students' educational experiences. For instance, ChatGPT can be used to produce tailored learning materials, interactive simulations, or automated language translation.

In conclusion, ChatGPT and other language models are extremely effective tools that can be used to improve learning, teaching, and research, even though they are not intended to take the place of actual professors and teachers. Instead of replacing human instruction, use these technologies properly and in tandem with it.

2.2.4 Fact: ChatGPT has a wide range of applications.

There are many possible uses for ChatGPT and other language models in numerous industries. Several instances include:

1. Business

For automated customer service, creating marketing material, market research, and trend analysis, ChatGPT

Stock market forecasting, sentiment analysis, investment analysis, named entity recognition and relation extraction from financial news and reports, as well as financial forecasting.

2. Healthcare

Medical diagnosis and treatment planning, individualised health advice, medical research, report and summary generation, and information extraction from electronic health records are all possible with ChatGPT.

3. Law

Legal research, contract analysis, document summaries, the creation of legal pleadings, and court filings can all be done with ChatGPT.

4. Engineering and science

Scientific publications and journals can use ChatGPT for named entity recognition, data analysis, technical description, summary, and more.

5. Humanities

Literature analysis, historical investigation, and language translation are all possible using ChatGPT.

Although there are many applications for ChatGPT and other language models, it is important to remember that they are not always a substitute for human knowledge. They can be used to supplement and improve current procedures and workflows, but they shouldn't be trusted to make important decisions on their own without supervision.

2.2.5 Reality: ChatGPT is available and open-sourced.

The fact that ChatGPT and other language models are open-sourced and available to a wide variety of users is one of their main advantages. Everyone has access to the code, which they can use to create their models and apps.

GitHub, a website for sharing and working together on code, is one of the key ways that ChatGPT and other language models are open-sourced. Users can obtain the code for ChatGPT and other language models on GitHub, where they can also participate in the model's development by submitting pull requests.

To construct models and applications utilising ChatGPT and other language models, there are a variety of tutorials and guides that offer detailed guidance. These tutorials and guidelines cover a wide range of topics, such as data preprocessing, model training, and application development, and they are made to be understandable by users with varied degrees of technical knowledge.

Some companies, like OpenAI, also offer access to pre-trained models via API and cloud services, allowing users to start developing models and applications without having to train and optimise the model themselves.

Additionally, because ChatGPT and other language models are open-source, they are simple to incorporate into already-existing systems and applications, allowing for the usage of these tools in a variety of settings.

In conclusion, users can easily create their models and applications because ChatGPT and other language models are open-sourced and accessible. Users with various degrees of technical expertise can begin utilising these tools because of the abundance of tutorials and guidelines that are available, as well as the access to pre-trained models through API.

2.3 The AI-Enabled Workforce and ChatGPT

ChatGPT is a useful instrument for higher education, but we need to be aware of its myths and realities. ChatGPT is a helpful support tool that may help with a variety of activities, even though it is true that it cannot take the place of real teachers and professors. Despite issues with prejudice and security, ChatGPT is open-sourced, and accessible to non-technical users, and it is always being improved. It may be applied to many different sectors and is most effective when used in conjunction with human skills. In general, ChatGPT can improve learning and facilitate it in novel ways.

Additionally, ChatGPT may help students get ready for jobs that use AI. Understanding and being able to deal with AI systems will become more crucial in many areas as technology develops. Students can acquire the abilities required to use AI efficiently in their future employment by integrating ChatGPT into higher education curricula.

ChatGPT, for instance, can be used to provide interactive, individualised learning. This can aid in the improvement of pupils' communication, analytical, and critical thinking abilities. Furthermore, ChatGPT can help with a variety of jobs like language translation, natural language processing, and data analysis—all of which are in great demand now and in the future.

Additionally, ChatGPT can be used to develop chatbots and virtual assistants, offering students practical experience in the development and design of these AI systems. This can provide students with a greater knowledge of the technology underlying AI as well as the moral and societal ramifications of its application.

In conclusion, ChatGPT can offer beneficial educational opportunities for students, preparing them for an AI-enabled workforce by giving them the abilities and information required to use AI successfully in their future employment. As a result, they will have a competitive advantage in the labour market and will be better equipped to work in industries that will be impacted by the use of AI technology.

Chapter Overview

ChatGPT and other language simulations can help with teaching and learning, but they cannot take the place of real instructors and professors. Instead of replacing human educators, ChatGPT should be used to support them. It is shown that ChatGPT has a wide range of capabilities and possible uses, dispelling the assumption that it is only helpful for straightforward tasks. Additionally, ChatGPT is growing more accurate and effective at managing a larger variety of inputs and queries as it continuously develops in areas like natural language interpretation, machine learning, and data processing. To avoid academic misconduct due to plagiarism issues, proper disclosure notice and/or reference of the model's output should be supplied.

CHAPTER THREE

HOW TO GET STARTED

This chapter will walk you through the process of getting started with ChatGPT and learning how to use it effectively for writing and communication. We will go over the fundamentals of installing and configuring ChatGPT. This chapter will provide you with the knowledge and resources you need to start using ChatGPT with confidence and ease, whether you are a student, educator, or professional. This chapter provides an overview of how to use ChatGPT to improve your writing and communication skills. So, let's get this party started!

3.1 A Step-by-Step Beginner's Guide

ChatGPT, created by OpenAI, is a powerful language model that can be accessed via a browser interface. To get started with ChatGPT, you must first create an OpenAI account. Because the platform is currently in beta, some instability is to be expected. When registering for an account, there may be a waitlist.

To create an OpenAI account, navigate your browser to https://openai.com/ and sign up for an account.

Once you have an OpenAI account, go to the ChatGPT browser interface: https://chat.openai.com/chat.

ChatGPT's interface resembles a browser within a browser. A large input field is located near the bottom of the screen. This is the input field where you will enter your ChatGPT prompts. Copy and paste the following text into the input field:

Contrast ChatGPT with the invention of the printing press.

After that, press return or click the arrow to the right of the input field. Congratulations if this was your first ChatGPT prompt! ChatGPT displays the output above the input field. Because this is an interactive conversation, you can respond to ChatGPT in the same way you would to a person. You could, for example, ask a follow-up question or engage in dialogue. You could also request that the previous response be revised, such as written for a different audience or purpose, described from a different perspective, with examples, and so on. In the following chapter, we will discuss how to create effective prompts. This chapter will concentrate on getting started with ChatGPT.

You can enter any text you want, and here are some more ChatGPT prompts:

"Write an essay about the value of education."

"Explain the concept of neural networks in a nutshell "

The ChatGPT browser interface can also be used to train the model on specific tasks or to fine-tune the model using your data. To train the model, you'll need to feed it a dataset of input-output pairs. This type of dataset is known as a "prompt." For example, you could give the model a prompt that consists of a question followed by an answer. Once trained, the model will be able to generate responses to similar questions.

It is worth noting that the server may occasionally reach capacity or the model may become unstable. If this occurs, try refreshing your browser, opening a new window, or attempting again later. It is also recommended that you have a stable internet connection to get the most out of your ChatGPT experience.

3.2 Getting Started with ChatGPT for Writing and Communication

ChatGPT is a flexible language model that can be used for a variety of tasks such as writing assistance, communication practice, and personalised learning.

Co-writing with AI is a new skill that can take time to master, particularly for those who have spent their careers staring at a blank page. It's critical to remember that ChatGPT is a tool that can be used to supplement and enhance the writing process, not replace it. Students will learn how to interact with ChatGPT for increased writing efficacy and efficiency with practice.

One way to begin using ChatGPT for writing is to generate writing prompts. A teacher, for example, can use ChatGPT to generate a list of creative writing prompts for students to use as inspiration for writing assignments. This can be an excellent way to encourage students to think outside the box and incorporate novel ideas into their writing.

Another way to use ChatGPT to help with writing is to summarise long texts. A student, for example, can use ChatGPT to summarise a lengthy research paper or news article, making it easier to comprehend and study. This can be an excellent way to help students comprehend complex texts while also saving time when researching.

Here are a few examples of writing prompts that might be used to generate various forms of writing to show the writing capabilities of ChatGPT:

"Publish a news story about the newest advances in AI technology."

To provide students with better knowledge of the subject, ChatGPT can be used to create a news article on the most recent developments in AI technology.

"Describe the Taj Mahal in your essay"

Students can gain a thorough grasp of the Taj Mahal by using ChatGPT to generate a descriptive essay on it.

“Write a convincing essay supporting the use of solar power.”

Students can learn about the possible advantages of solar energy and the justifications for why it should be used more frequently by using ChatGPT to create a persuasive essay promoting its use.

The output of the model won’t always be flawless, therefore it’s always a smart idea to have a person evaluate the output to make sure it is correct and pertinent. To guarantee that the output matches the input, it is also essential to incorporate high-quality, diverse data when training the model.

CHAPTER FOUR

SUCCESSFUL PROMPTS

The broad guidelines and practical promoting techniques for using ChatGPT in a professional situation will be covered in this chapter. Students will produce more precise and pertinent material from ChatGPT by following these guidelines and techniques. Students who comprehend these ideas will be able to use ChatGPT to write, research, and finish assignments quickly and effectively.

4.1 Prompting Principles

Follow these general guidelines while using ChatGPT to create text to receive the most precise and pertinent results.

4.1.1 Pick Your Words Wisely

Keep in mind that ChatGPT cannot read your mind, so be specific and concise with your prompts. For instance, the request "Can you cite this" does not result in a citation, whereas the request "Can you arrange this as a citation" does.

Additionally, it's critical to give precise and understandable instructions when requesting information because the model is unable to deduce the context or meaning of ambiguous or confusing queries. This necessitates being clear and concise while giving ChatGPT instructions. For instance, you might say, "Revise this paragraph to incorporate more information about the benefits of exercise," as opposed to merely asking, "Can you change this paragraph?"

4.1.2 Establish the Conversation's Goal and Focus

Before anything else, it's critical to specify the aim and focus of the discussion or content that you want ChatGPT to generate. This will ensure that the output is pertinent to your needs and assist the model in being directed in the proper direction. For instance, if you want ChatGPT to create an article about the advantages of exercising, you should ask them to do so at the beginning of the conversation.

4.1.3 Be Clear and Brief

Another crucial rule is to be clear and succinct while giving instructions to ChatGPT. To ensure that the model understands exactly what you want it to accomplish, be clear and specific in your prompts. For instance, you might say, "Revise this paragraph to incorporate more information about the benefits of exercise," as opposed to merely asking, "Can you change this paragraph?"

Additionally, it's crucial to only enter data that is pertinent to the text or conversation. Asking too many open-ended or wide questions can provide outcomes that are irrelevant or unclear. Additionally, it's a good idea to refrain from asking too many personal inquiries, like "how are you?" because the model can't understand or answer them.

4.1.4 Provide Background

To make sure that the model's responses are correct and pertinent, it can be helpful to provide context for the discussion or text. For instance, you may describe your position ("I'm a marketing expert who helps firms enhance their online presence"), the target audience ("I'm writing this for a group of small business owners"), and the desired tone ("I'm writing this for a group of small business owners") (e.g. "I want this to sound informative and persuasive"). This might aid in making sure that the text produced by the model is suitable for the target market and purpose.

e.g. "I'm an X who helps Y do Z. Can you provide me with an A for B that explains C in a D manner? ".

4.1.5 Demand more

Another important idea is to encourage ChatGPT to elaborate on its responses by giving suggestions and requesting more details. This will enable the model to produce text that is more precise and detailed. To create an email asking someone whether they are interested in a product, for instance, you may ask the model to "rewrite the above email so it sounds more persuasive."

4.1.6 Maintain the Topic of Conversation

Use the "stop" command to end the current action if the conversation or text veers off-topic or becomes irrelevant. A steady connection to the server can occasionally be restored by restarting the browser or typing "go on."

Keep the talk on the topic, evaluate and rewrite, give feedback, and make sure you get what you want. This will make it easier to guarantee that the result is correct and appropriate for your purposes.

4.2 Prompting Techniques

There are several tactics you may employ while using ChatGPT to create text to influence the model's output and obtain the most precise and pertinent results.

4.2.1 Take on a certain persona or viewpoint

It can be useful to specify a specific persona or perspective when requesting ChatGPT to write about or discuss a subject. For instance, you may instruct ChatGPT to "write from the standpoint of a customer reviewing a new product" or "act as a marketing professional and highlight the benefits of social media advertising." This might aid in ensuring that the content produced by the model is pertinent and suitable for the target market and purpose.

4.2.2 Layer Inquiries

Layer Prompts to Guide ChatGPT: You can direct ChatGPT's responses to be more pertinent and helpful by giving it precise directions on what to do. You might ask ChatGPT to, for instance, "Please summarise this article," "Please make this sound more engaging," or "revise to additionally consider x." The model can produce language that is more pertinent to the task at hand if you give it precise directions like "Revise that to add quotes or examples, or refer to an idea."

4.2.3 The Matrix Method

Utilizing the matrix method, which entails first questioning ChatGPT about one issue and then how another topic relates to it, is another successful tactic. By doing so, you may ensure that the content is more coherent and that the model's output is more focused. You may instruct ChatGPT to, for instance, "Write about the advantages of exercise and how it pertains to mental health."

4.3 Exporting from ChatGPT

Respecting the institution's regulations on academic integrity is essential while using ChatGPT or other language models in a higher education setting. This means that ChatGPT should only be used when it is allowed by school policies and that in cases where ChatGPT is prohibited, other resources should be used instead.

The company that created the model's IP and usage policies must also be followed. These policies describe how the model should be used properly and any constraints or limits that should be taken into account.

It is advised to use ChatGPT in conjunction with other resources, such as textbooks and academic publications, to develop a more comprehensive understanding of a subject. Through this method, the topic can be better understood, and any data produced by the model can be independently verified.

Lastly, be honest about how you use ChatGPT and other language models. This guarantees openness and comprehension of the tool's limits. The school is employing these technologies to improve the educational experience, and any information produced by the model is not meant to replace the expert opinion or professional judgement, according to a proposed notification.

Summary

We talked about several guidelines for acquiring the most precise and pertinent information from ChatGPT. This chapter highlighted the importance of carefully selecting your words, defining the dialogue with purpose and focus, being precise and succinct, offering context, inspiring ChatGPT to elaborate on its responses, and maintaining the flow of the conversation. It also discusses the efficient ChatGPT prompting techniques, such as requesting the model to write or discuss a subject from a certain persona or perspective.

CHAPTER FIVE

USE OF CHATGPT IN WRITING

The different methods that ChatGPT can help with the writing process are explored in Chapter 5, "Writing with ChatGPT. This chapter will examine the possibilities of this potent language model to enhance writing, from grammar checking and proofreading to summarising and creative writing. The chapter will also go into using ChatGPT for individualised writing courses and brainstorming, offering advice on how to use this technology for writing.

5.1 Text Summarization, Grammar Checking, Proofreading, and Editing

5.1.1 Checking Your Grammar

There are various methods to use ChatGPT to proofread student writing for grammar and punctuation. The most popular application is as a grammar and spell checker. This can be accomplished by utilising a language model that has been trained on a sizable dataset of text that has proper grammar and spelling to analyse student work and indicate any faults.

For instance, a teacher might use a dataset of student writings that have been assessed and revised to train a ChatGPT model. The model can then be used to review fresh essays created by pupils and highlight any grammatical and punctuation mistakes. The teacher can then go over the errors that were highlighted and give the pupil feedback.

Using pre-trained models that have already been trained on sizable text datasets is another option to leverage ChatGPT and other language models for grammar checking. To enhance the performance and accuracy of these models, a smaller dataset of student writing can be used. The model can be trained on a dataset of student writing with known faults, and its performance can then be assessed on a different dataset of student writing.

By giving students automated feedback on their writing, ChatGPT and other language models can be used to teach students grammar and punctuation in addition to grammar and spelling. A model might be taught to point out typical grammatical errors like subject-verb agreement or sentence structure, for instance. Students can use this to recognise and fix their own mistakes, gradually increasing their writing abilities.

The capacity of ChatGPT and other language models to handle vast volumes of data fast and accurately is one advantage of utilising them for grammar checking. This qualifies them for the analysis of a huge volume of student writing samples and enables teachers to give students more in-depth and individualised feedback.

Although ChatGPT and other language models can be helpful resources for grammar checking, they shouldn't be used in place of real teachers or editors. These simulations are prone to errors and might not be able to properly comprehend the purpose and context of student writing. As a result, it's crucial to combine them with human skill and judgement.

In conclusion, grammar and punctuation checking in student writing can be done using ChatGPT and other language models. They can be used to provide automatic feedback, check for grammar and spelling, and assist students in learning grammar and punctuation. It's crucial to keep in mind that these models should be utilised in conjunction with human discretion and knowledge.

Examples of ChatGPT questions:

Please proofread this sentence's punctuation and grammar: "John and I went to the store."

"What are some typical grammar errors in this passage: The cat was sitting on the mat. Huge and fluffy, it was a big cat. It had smooth, silky fur."

Please comment on this essay's grammar and punctuation on the subject of "the value of education."

Please be aware that the sample prompts are only intended to show how ChatGPT can be used for grammar checking; the actual results may differ based on the training data and model tuning.

5.1.2 Editing and checking for errors

The domain of editing and proofreading student writing is one of the most promising uses of ChatGPT and other language models in higher education. These tools can help students and teachers improve the calibre and clarity of written work as well as spot and fix grammar and spelling flaws as well as other problems that may lessen the writing's overall effectiveness.

By educating ChatGPT on a corpus of student writing, for instance, the model can be used for editing and proofreading. After being trained, the model can be used to make suggestions for different wording and structuring for certain passages of text. The model, for instance, can propose other words or sentence structures to help improve the coherence and clarity of the argument if a student is having trouble writing a short and clear thesis statement.

Consider the following three sample questions and an illustration of a section of writing before and after ChatGPT editing for word choice, clarity, and narrative flow to show the tool's potential for proofreading and editing.

1. Clarity and conciseness are improved

The following sentence needs to be clarified and condensed, so if you can, change it to read: "The study, which was conducted by a team of researchers from multiple universities, sought to investigate the impact of social media on mental health among young adults, and the results of the study were quite surprising."

Result

The study, which was directed by academics from multiple universities, examined the link between young adults' psychological well-being and social media and came up with unexpected results.

2. Different word choices

The following line needs to be made more interesting by using different words than "The lecture covered a lot of material, yet it was dry and uninspiring."

Result

"The presentation covered a wide range of issues, yet it was dull and unimpressive."

3. enhancing flow

For better narrative flow, rewrite the following sentence as follows: "The study, which was undertaken by a team of academics from several universities, attempted to evaluate the impact of social media on mental health among young adults, and the results of the study were fairly surprising.

Result

"According to research, using social media could be bad for young adults' mental health. It is also known that there is a complex and poorly understood relationship between social media use and mental health. To fully understand how social media affects mental health and to identify effective ways to help young adults, more research is necessary."

According to the study, social media use might be detrimental to mental health, especially in young adults.

But it also showed how complicated and poorly understood the connection between social media use and mental health is.

To completely comprehend the connection between social media and mental health and to create successful treatments to support young adults, further research is required.

This example shows how ChatGPT may help with proofreading and editing student writing by recommending different word choices, phrases, and sentence structures to enhance the clarity, concision, and narrative flow of written work. This can help students write better and more effectively, and it can also help teachers give comments and guidance to students more effectively.

By including the model in a writing programme or platform, ChatGPT can also be utilised for editing and proofreading. This enables instructors to quickly analyse and modify a significant volume of student work as well as give students feedback and ideas as they write in real-time

Additionally, instructors and institutions can save time and resources by using ChatGPT to help with the automatic grading and scoring of written assignments.

While ChatGPT and other language models can be highly beneficial for editing and proofreading student writing, they shouldn't be utilised in place of human editing and feedback. Although these tools can be useful for finding mistakes and problems, they might not always be able to comprehend the context and intent of the work. For the most accurate and efficient outcomes, it is crucial to combine human editing and feedback with ChatGPT and other language models.

5.1.3 Text Summarization

Text summarization is another area in higher education where ChatGPT and other language models can be extremely helpful. Instructors and administrators can rapidly understand the main ideas and themes of a document by using these tools to swiftly and effectively summarise student writing. Students can also benefit from text summarising since it allows them to focus on the most crucial information while also helping them to summarise and understand difficult materials.

By putting ChatGPT through a corpus of student writing, for instance, the model can be trained to perform text summarization. After being trained, the model can be used to produce a summary of a particular document or section of text. As a result, the model can be used to create a summary of a student's research paper that highlights the most important conclusions and arguments, which will help an instructor rapidly grasp the essential aspects of the work.

Consider the following three sample prompts and a demonstration of a prompt that summarises a passage of text to show the possibilities of ChatGPT for text summarization:

"Please offer a summary of the research paper below on how young adults' mental health is affected by social media."

"Please summarise the main ideas covered in the lecture on the history of the American Civil War that is coming up."

"Please offer a summary of the key points and information included in the article below about how climate change affects ocean ecosystems."

By creating a summary of a particular document or passage of text, ChatGPT can be used to summarise student writing and extract key themes, as this example shows. This can help teachers and administrators focus on the most crucial information while also saving time and resources for students.

It's crucial to remember that the summaries produced by the algorithm might not always be accurate and should be checked by a person.

5.2 ChatGPT for Writing Creatively

A few instances of the many creative writing uses for ChatGPT are as follows:

1. Creation of stories

ChatGPT can create an entire story from only a single statement or request. For instance,

"A young princess once lived in a kingdom far, far away and was afflicted by a cruel witch."

2. Poetry creation

Poetry can be produced with ChatGPT with some tweaking.

"Create a poem that addresses love and loss."

3. creation of dialogue

A script or story's dialogue can be created with ChatGPT.

Write an exchange between two friends in which they discuss their future goals.

4. Character spoofing

ChatGPT can be adjusted to mimic the voice of a well-known author.

"Create a short narrative in Ernest Hemingway's style."

5. Writing song lyrics

Song lyrics can also be produced via ChatGPT.

"Compose a song about a heartbreak"

6. Creation of a screenplay

A movie or television show's screenplay can be generated through ChatGPT.

"Write a comedy script about some pals going on a road trip."

7. Literary nonfiction

Additionally, ChatGPT can be utilised to produce creative nonfiction writing.

"Describe how you overcame a phobia in a personal essay."

8. Fanliterature

Fanfiction can also be created with ChatGPT.

"Create a fanfiction about Harry Potter with Hermione as the primary character," was the request.

These are just a few instances of the many ways that ChatGPT may be used to inspire creative writing. With the correct prompts, it can also inspire a variety of writing styles.

Be aware that ChatGPT may produce work that is not fully original or unique because the model was trained on a big corpus of text. The quality of the input data and any particular model fine-tuning will also affect the output data quality.

When using ChatGPT-generated content, take into account the moral and legal ramifications. For instance, it's crucial to confirm that you have the legal authority to do so and that the content does not violate any existing copyrights or trademarks before using ChatGPT to create content that you intend to publish or sell.

Additionally, it's crucial to realise that the model may produce text with offensive or biased language because it was trained on material from the internet, which may contain those examples.

Another thing to keep in mind is that, even though the model has been tailored to a particular task, the output produced by ChatGPT is not always flawless and requires human supervision and editing.

Last but not least, it's critical to keep in mind that ChatGPT is a tool, and the outcomes it produces need to be used as inspiration rather than as a substitute for human ingenuity. The model can assist spark creativity and jump-start the writing process, but a human writer should still craft and polish the final piece.

5.3 Brainstorming via ChatGPT

Even though ChatGPT and other language models are frequently considered to be tools for editing and proofreading, they can also be used in several inventive and original ways to improve students' writing abilities. Students can improve their writing by using these tools to come up with fresh ideas, brainstorm, and construct outlines.

By using the model to come up with fresh ideas for writing assignments, for instance, students can use ChatGPT to help them with their writing. A student who is having trouble coming up with a topic for a marketing case study, for instance, can utilise a prompt like "Please generate three prospective case study themes on how social media marketing affects customer behaviour" to come up with a list of options.

Students can also utilise ChatGPT to develop ideas for a particular topic by using the model as a brainstorming tool. To come up with ideas, a student preparing a marketing strategy, for instance, could utilise a prompt like "Please produce a list of five viable techniques for a social media marketing campaign for a new e-commerce platform."

You can utilise ChatGPT to draught project outlines as well. To create a structured strategy for the case study, a student working on one might utilise a suggestion like, "Please produce an outline for a case study on the impact of social media marketing on customer behaviour."

Consider the following sample prompts that show creative ways to use ChatGPT to illustrate the possibilities of ChatGPT for writing assistance:

“Please suggest three case study subjects on how social media marketing has affected consumer behaviour”.

“Please come up with a list of five possible social media marketing campaign methods for a new e-commerce platform.”

"Can you please create a case study outline on the effects of social media marketing on consumer behaviour?"

It's crucial to remember that these ChatGPT usage examples are not restricted to these prompts and can be applied in a variety of other contexts to meet the needs of the learner.

5.4 Writing Instruction with ChatGPT

To help teachers create lesson plans, ChatGPT and other language models can be used in a variety of inventive and original ways. These technologies can be used to design lesson plans, write educational materials, take quizzes and tests, and save time and effort for teachers while giving students compelling learning opportunities.

By using the model to compile a set of learning objectives, activities, and assessments for a specific topic, instructors can utilise ChatGPT to develop lesson plans. For instance, to create a structured plan for the lesson, a teacher of a marketing course could ask their students to "please prepare a lesson plan on the impact of social media marketing on customer behaviour."

Teachers can also use ChatGPT by using the model to make tests and quizzes for their classes. For instance, to create a list of questions and answers for the quiz, a teacher of a history course would ask, "Please build a multiple-choice quiz on the reasons for for the American Civil War."

Writing instructional materials like handouts or study guides is another usage for ChatGPT. To create a structured guide for the students, a teacher instructing a course on literature would give a prompt such, as "Please produce a study guide on the themes and symbols featured in the novel 'The Great Gatsby'."

Consider the following sample prompts that show creative applications of ChatGPT to illustrate the potential of ChatGPT for generating educational content:

"Create a lesson plan on how social media marketing affects consumer behaviour, please."

"Create a multiple-choice test about the reasons for the American Civil War, please."

"Create a study guide on the ideas and symbolism found in "The Great Gatsby" please."

It's crucial to remember that these ChatGPT use examples are not limited to these prompts and can be applied in a variety of various ways to suit the requirements of the educator.

Summary

The extensive language model ChatGPT has several uses, such as editing, proofreading, and grammar checking for student work. It can either be fine-tuned on a smaller dataset of student writing to increase its accuracy or trained on a large dataset of text with proper grammar and spelling to analyse student writing and indicate faults. It can also be used to give pupils automated feedback and aid them in learning grammar and punctuation. Use ChatGPT in addition to human wisdom and discretion.

Additionally, ChatGPT can be used for a variety of creative writing tasks, including the creation of stories, poems, dialogue, character impersonations, song lyrics, screenplays, creative non-fiction, and fan fiction

But be aware that because the model was trained on a sizable body of text, it might produce results that aren't fully original or unique.

The quality of the input data and the precise model fine-tuning will also influence the output's quality.

Remember that model is a tool, and the output it produces should be utilised as inspiration and not as a replacement for human creativity. Take into account the moral and legal ramifications of employing ChatGPT-generated content.

CHAPTER SIX

CHATGPT FOR COMMUNICATION

We explore the numerous ways that ChatGPT and other language models can be used to improve communication in higher education in this chapter. We examine the many ChatGPT functions for communications, from conversation simulation to vocabulary learning and natural language understanding to professional communication and content creation.

6.1 Dialogue Simulation

The potential of ChatGPT and other language models to replicate discussions in higher education is one of their most promising uses. Some examples include allowing students to practise conversational roles in conversationally realistic settings that are adapted to their learning needs, learning a new skill or role, a new subject or field of inquiry, or speaking in a foreign language. These language models can provide responses that are comparable to what a native speaker would say by being trained on a lot of data, including transcripts of actual conversations.

The creation of a virtual language partner for students to practise speaking with is one application for conversation simulation. A student might enter a query or statement in a foreign language, for instance, and the language model would answer appropriately or pose a follow-up question. As a result, students can practise speaking and listen in a low-pressure environment where they can make mistakes and get feedback without worrying about looking foolish.

Making a virtual language instructor who can provide students with individualised feedback and corrections is another application. For instance, if a student entered a sentence in a foreign language, the language model would correct it and offer advice on how to make it better. Students can do this to get real-time feedback on their language proficiency, which will help them advance more quickly.

The creation of artificial settings that promote language immersion through dialogue simulation is a final use case. A student may enter a query or remark in a foreign language, for instance, and the language model would answer appropriately or ask follow-up questions as though the student were taking part in a discussion. This enables students to practise speaking and listening in a more immersed environment, which may be more beneficial for improving fluency.

Examples of ChatGPT conversation simulation prompts:

"What do you prefer to do when you're not working?"

"What is your favourite holiday custom, please?"

"What do you believe to be the largest issue your nation is now facing?"

In all of these use case examples, ChatGPT can assist students in honing their conversational abilities by producing answers to their prompts, which can teach them how to carry on a conversation and react correctly in various scenarios.

For instance, if a student enters the command "Generate a chat between two friends discussing the most recent political news," ChatGPT will produce a conversation that goes like this:

"Friend 1: Are you aware of the recently proposed new laws?

Friend 2: What's going on, no?

They're attempting to enact a law that would limit voting rights, says Friend 1.

Friend 2: That's awful; we must ensure that we remain aware and take action to stop it."

In conclusion, using ChatGPT and other language simulation tools in higher education can be a very effective way to assist students to develop their language abilities. Students may benefit from a low-stakes, individualised, and immersive experience to increase their language fluency through the opportunity to imitate real-world discussions with virtual language partners.

6.2 Vocabulary Development

The development of one's vocabulary is an important part of learning a language, and ChatGPT can help in several ways. To provide results that include new vocabulary items and their definitions, these models can be trained using a lot of data, such as language dictionaries and text corpora.

To assist pupils in memorising new terms, creating flashcards and tests is one application for vocabulary acquisition. The language model might, for instance, reply to a student's input of a vocabulary term by providing the word's meaning, an example sentence, and a synonym or antonym. As a result, students can obtain feedback on their development while practising their vocabulary retention in a low-stakes environment.

Using ChatGPT and other language models to offer in-the-moment translation support is another use case. As an illustration, if a learner inputs a statement in their native tongue, the language model will provide the translation in the target language. This enables students who are reading or writing in a foreign language to evaluate their grasp and advance their comprehension, which might be valuable for them.

The provision of customised vocabulary lists and exercises using ChatGPT and other language models is a final use case. The language model might, for instance, respond to a student's input with a list of pertinent vocabulary items and tasks to learn them. For a more effective learning process, this enables students to concentrate on the language that is most pertinent to their needs and interests.

Examples of ChatGPT prompts for learning new words:

"Can you explain what the word "perplexed" means?"

“Could you translate, "I‘m heading to the store," into Spanish?”

“Can you provide me with a list of computer science-related vocabulary words?”

In conclusion, ChatGPT and other language models can be effective tools for helping students in higher education learn new words. The creation of flashcards, quizzes, real-time translation, and customised vocabulary lists and activities can all help students retain vocabulary and enhance their understanding and fluency.

6.3 Understanding Natural Language

The capacity of language models like ChatGPT to comprehend and produce natural language is one of its primary features. This ability can be used to improve natural language comprehension in several different ways, such as through comprehending idiomatic statements and spotting cultural allusions.

6.3.1 Idiomatic Expressions

Understanding idiomatic expressions are one possible application for ChatGPT in natural language comprehension. For instance, a learner may type an idiomatic expression into a ChatGPT-powered tool, and the tool would explain what "let the cat out of the bag" means. Students learning a new language or those who are not familiar with colloquial terms in their native tongue may find this to be especially helpful.

6.3.2 Recognizing Cultural References

Recognizing cultural allusions is another potential use case.

The tool would display details about the reference and its cultural context once a learner entered a passage of text containing a cultural allusion. Students who are studying literature or learning about other cultures may find this to be extremely useful.

A third use case for ChatGPT is sentiment analysis, a method for locating arbitrary information in the source text. Understanding consumer reviews, posts on social media, and news stories may be aided by this.

There are three examples of ChatGPT prompts for NLU:

“GDefinethe idiom "let the cat out of the bag" please.”

"If possible, please elaborate on the cultural allusion made in this: He was insane."

“’I had a dreadful experience at this restaurant,‘ this text's sentiment, please.”

ChatGPT can help with natural language understanding, but it is not a perfect solution and shouldn't take the place of human comprehension. Furthermore, it is critical to recognise that language models like ChatGPT are trained on a big dataset, which can introduce biases and make them less likely to recognise specific cultural allusions or idiomatic idioms. Natural language processing researchers are now studying this topic.

6.3.3 Enhancing Listening Skills

By listening to the created discourse and responding or reacting properly, students can exercise and enhance their listening skills by using ChatGPT to generate various scenarios.

For instance, a pupil can enter the prompt "ChatGPT will answer to a request to "generate a discussion between a client and a customer service representative" by presenting a dialogue like "Customer: My order was delivered, but one item is missing. Could you please aid me in this? Customer service agent: I'm sorry this has caused you trouble. I need your order number so I can look into this for you. Could you kindly give it to me? Customer:

A23456. Customer service agent: Thank you; I now understand the problem. I'll mail that thing your way straight immediately "

6.3.4 Enhancing Non-Verbal Communication

Through visualising the generated discourse, students can practise and develop their non-verbal communication abilities, such as facial expressions, gestures, and posture, using ChatGPT.

With the prompt "Generate a scenario of a job interview," for instance, a student can enter a dialogue like "Interviewer: Can you tell me about your experience in this field? Interviewee:

(Nodding with assurance) "Yes, I have a lot of expertise in this area. I have experience working on a variety of projects and have a solid grasp of the market.

6.4 Content Development

Various other communication duties that are now typical for professionals in numerous professions can also be aided by ChatGPT. Other tasks involving professional communication and corresponding ChatGPT prompts include:

1. Business correspondence

By offering advice on appropriate language, tone, and formatting for use in creating reports, memos, and other business documents, ChatGPT can help students gain the skills necessary for effective business communication.

For illustration, a pupil could answer the question:

"Write a message detailing the status of a current project to the executive team of the organisation."

Result :

"To Management Team," the outcome in the name of

Subject: Project X Progress Update The team's work on Project X has advanced significantly as of [date]. We have achieved the goals mentioned in the original proposal, and we are on schedule to finish the project by the deadline. Important achievements to date include:

- Completion of market analysis and research
- Creation of a thorough project plan
- Getting the staff and resources you need
- Execution of significant project milestones and tasks

We will concentrate on the following duties going forward:

- Constant monitoring and project plan modifications as necessary
- Close coordination with all parties involved will result in successful execution.
- Regular management team progress reports"

2. Email and letter writing

ChatGPT can help students write formal emails and letters by offering formatting, tone, and language suggestions.

For illustration, a pupil could answer the question:

"Create a business email to ask to meet with a possible employer."

Result

"Greetings, [Employer] I hope you are well and reading my email. I'm writing to let you know that I'd be interested in meeting with you to talk about prospective employment prospects with your business. I have a particular interest in the [job] role, and I feel that my knowledge and expertise meet the needs of the position "

3. Producing customised answers to consumer questions or support requests.

"Create a customised response to the following client query regarding a product's return policy: "I purchased the XYZ product, but it is not functioning properly. Can I send it back? "

"Create a chatbot script for a customer support platform that responds to typical queries and issues with a certain service, like "How do I modify my membership plan?"

4. Creating email or message templates for advertising or sales efforts:

"Write a 2-minute explainer video screenplay about the advantages of a particular commodity or service, such "as The advantages of adopting DEF technology for your business."

"Create a conversation flow for a chatbot that would help people looking for particular kinds of employment, like "Searching for a job in the field of XYZ."

5. Social media and online communication: By offering tips on tone, phrasing, and netiquette, ChatGPT may help students learn how to communicate effectively on social media and online platforms.

For instance, if a student enters the prompt "Generate a tweet regarding a recent news report," ChatGPT will send out a tweet that reads something like "Just read about the new #climatechange policy being proposed - this is an important step in the correct direction for our world #sustainable."

6. Creating social media captions or posts for brands or people.

"In a social media post, please summarise the key ideas from the article "The Future of Artificial Intelligence" in no more than 280 characters."

"Create discussion starters for a teambuilding activity that focuses on collaboration and communication for a particular business, like "Improving communication in the tech industry."

7. Building autonomous chatbots for e-commerce or customer support platforms:

"Create an email template with the subject line "Introducing our new ABC software for small businesses" for a sales campaign aimed at small businesses."

"Create a social media post for a clothing firm introducing a new product with a targeted audience, such "as New arrivals for the fashion-forward professional."

8. Production of speech

Students can learn how to organise and deliver a good oral presentation by using ChatGPT, which can produce speeches or oral presentations on a specified topic.

For instance, a pupil can enter the question "Create a five-minute speech highlighting the value of education, and ChatGPT will provide a speech with statements like "Education is the cornerstone upon which we construct our futures. It is the secret to realising our potential and accomplishing our objectives."

9. Creating material for virtual assistants or chatbots:

"Create a series of answers for a virtual assistant that can aid with appointment scheduling, such as "How can I help you plan your next appointment?"

"Make a conversation flow for a chatbot that will aid with customer service questions like "How can I help you with your purchase today?"

10. Writing scripts for podcasts or videos:

"Create questions for a self-reflection journaling exercise on values and aspirations for a particular profession or job, like "Reflecting on my values and ambitions as a teacher."

"Create discussion starters for a therapy session that focuses on managing stress and anxiety for a particular population, such as "Managing stress for working mothers."

11. Coming up with discussion starters for networking or team-building activities:

Create discussion starters for a team-building activity that focuses on communication and trust, such as "Discussing approaches to create trust within the team."

"Come up with a list of conversation starters for a networking event that is all about connecting people and networking, such "as How to make a lasting impression at a networking event?"."

The potential for ChatGPT and other language models to be significant in educating students for an AI-enabled workforce cannot be understated. Students must build practical professional communication skills that are in demand in the job market as more and more industries integrate AI into their operations. Students can learn a wide range of applied professional communication skills, including business communication, social media and online communication, customer service, and content creation, with the aid of ChatGPT's capacity to generate personalised responses, automated chatbots, email and message templates, scripts, and conversation prompts. ChatGPT can be a useful tool for educators and students in developing a workforce that is AI-ready when used with the supervision of a human teacher and training data that is of high quality and diversity.

Chapter Summary

To enhance language learning and the development of professional communication skills, Chapter 6 examined the numerous ways that ChatGPT and other language models can be employed in higher education. The main emphasis is on using ChatGPT to simulate conversations, which enables students to hone their speaking and listening abilities in a natural environment. The creation of flashcards and tests to aid students in memorising new vocabulary words and the provision of real-time translation assistance are further used The use of ChatGPT for teaching professional communication skills is also covered in this chapter. Examples include generating questions and prompts, dialogue generation, vocabulary improvement, speech generation, email and letter writing, social media and online communication, and listening skill improvement. The chapter emphasises the advantages of adopting ChatGPT in various contexts, including the provision of low-stakes, individualised, and immersive experiences to enhance fluency and communication skills.

CHAPTER SEVEN

PERSONALIZED LEARNING

Individualized learning, adaptive testing, and intelligent tutoring/advising are the main topics of Chapter 7, "Individualized Learning," which explains how to improve the educational experience for all students, including those with impairments. Technology is used in personalised learning to adapt training to the particular requirements and skills of each student, making the learning process faster and more successful. With adaptive testing, test questions are changed in difficulty based on a student's performance, giving a more realistic picture of their level of understanding. Artificial intelligence is used in intelligent tutoring and counselling to give pupils individualised feedback and direction to enhance their learning. The topic of accommodations for students with impairments will also be covered, along with how ChatGPT might help these students meet their academic objectives. The final section of this chapter covers suggestions for using ChatGPT to encourage student collaboration.

7.1 Individualized Instruction

Personalized learning is the process of tailoring teaching and content to each student's particular needs and preferences. By giving students individualised information and training based on their performance and preferences, educators can use ChatGPT to create personalised learning experiences for their students.

Giving students tailored performance feedback is one way that ChatGPT can be utilised for personalised learning. When a student asks ChatGPT, for instance, "What areas do I need to improve on in my math class?", ChatGPT will provide detailed comments on the student's strengths and shortcomings. This enables the learner to concentrate on their areas for growth and raise their level of performance.

Giving students content that is based on their interests and preferences is another way that ChatGPT can be utilised for individualised learning. A student might inquire on ChatGPT, for instance, "Can you provide me with a list of suggested resources on the subject of "machine learning"?" based on the student's preferences and interests, ChatGPT would react with a list of resources that are most pertinent to and helpful.

Giving students individualised teaching based on their learning styles is the third way that ChatGPT may be utilised for personalised learning. A student might ask ChatGPT, for instance, "Can you explain the notion of "machine learning" in a way that is simple for me to understand?" and in response, ChatGPT would give a detailed explanation that was suited to the student's learning preferences.

Examples of ChatGPT questions:

“What is my math subject do I need to work on more? "Can you provide me with a list of the best books on machine learning‘?"

“Can you provide me an easy-to-understand explanation of the "machine learning" concept?”

These are just a few of the numerous instances of how teachers can use ChatGPT to tailor learning experiences for their pupils. These technologies can aid in enhancing student engagement, motivation, and learning outcomes by offering students content and teaching that is specifically suited to their needs and preferences based on their performance. Personalization is not a one-size-fits-all answer, though, and it should be used in conjunction with other instructional tactics and approaches for a more all-encompassing approach to education.

7.2 Adjustable Testing

Adaptive tests adjust to the student's level of understanding to give a more realistic picture of their abilities. By producing questions that are specific to the student's level of knowledge, language models like ChatGPT can be utilised to generate adaptive examinations.

Question generating is one possible application for ChatGPT in adaptive testing. For instance, a student may use a ChatGPT-powered application to take a pre-test, and based on their results, the tool would produce follow-up questions that are specific to their level of comprehension. Students who are having trouble with a particular subject or who require extra help to stay up with the class could find this to be especially helpful.

Question customisation is another possible use scenario. A test would be generated based on the student's degree of understanding of the subject once they entered it into the programme. Students who are self-studying or studying at their own pace may find this to be of particular use.

The creation of multiple-choice questions is a third use case. A text passage might be entered by a student, and the tool would then produce multiple-choice questions to assess the student's comprehension of the passage. This might be especially useful for students who are learning a new language or studying literature.

Three illustrations of ChatGPT questions for adaptive testing:

"Please come up with three follow-up inquiries based on the pre-test results for the learner."

"Please create a test depending on how well-versed the student is in the field of algebra."

"The passage "The cat sat on the mat" should inspire 5 multiple-choice questions, according to the requester."

7.3 Knowledgeable Tutoring and Counseling

Intelligent tutoring is the practice of using technology to give students individualised, step-by-step instruction and immediate feedback. By giving students individualised advice and feedback depending on their performance and needs, ChatGPT can be utilised to develop intelligent tutoring systems.

Giving pupils step-by-step instructions and feedback on problem-solving exercises is one way that ChatGPT can be utilised for intelligent tutoring. For instance, ChatGPT could reply to a student's request for assistance with a math issue by providing a series of instructions and comments. This enables the student to solve the issue at their own pace while getting any necessary direction and criticism.

Giving pupils immediate feedback on their comprehension of the subject matter is another way that ChatGPT can be utilised for intelligent instruction. To test a student's comprehension of the concept of "machine learning," for instance, a student may ask ChatGPT, "Can you test my grasp of that concept?" ChatGPT would then react with a series of questions to gauge the student's understanding and offer guidance on any areas of uncertainty.

A third way ChatGPT can be utilised for intelligent tutoring is to give students individualised study recommendations depending on how they are performing and what they need. A student might inquire on ChatGPT, for instance, "What sources should I consult to enhance my understanding of "machine learning"?" In response, ChatGPT would provide a list of suggested resources based on the student's performance and needs.

Typical ChatGPT Prompts:

"Can you assist me in resolving this math issue?"

"Can you check to see if I grasp the meaning of machine learning'?"

"What sources should I consult to deepen my comprehension of "machine learning"?"

It's critical to distinguish between intelligent tutoring and adaptive testing as well as personalised learning. Personalized learning is the process of tailoring teaching and content to each student's particular needs and preferences. The term "adaptive testing" describes the application of technology to deliver personalised evaluations and feedback based on student performance. Intelligent tutoring can be used in conjunction with personalised learning and adaptive testing, but its main goal is to give students step-by-step instructions and immediate feedback to help them comprehend and solve problems. Intelligent tutoring is a more sophisticated version of personalised learning and adaptive testing that uses technology to give students feedback and instruction that is specific to their performance and requirements. This makes learning more effective and efficient because it enables students to work through concepts and issues at their own pace while getting the help and feedback they require in real-time.

7.4 Arrangements for Students with Disabilities

A wide range of disabilities, including those affecting reading, writing, and communication, can be accommodated via ChatGPT. ChatGPT offers several accommodations for students with disabilities, such as:

1. Text-to-speech

Text-to-speech conversion is a feature of ChatGPT that can be useful for students who struggle with reading or vision. For this lodging, an illustration of a prompt would be:

Any section from a book or article could be used as the input text for "Read the following passage in a genuine voice."

2. Speech-to-text

ChatGPT can translate speech to text, which can be useful for students who have trouble speaking or moving. For this lodging, an illustration of a prompt would be:

"Translate the following audio recording," with the student's voiceover as the input.

3. text condensing

Text can be made simpler via ChatGPT, which is beneficial for pupils who have cognitive or learning challenges. For this lodging, an illustration of a prompt would be:

Any section from a book or article could be the input material for the instruction, "Simplify the following passage for a 5th-grade reading level."

4. Language interpreting

For students who are non-native speakers or who have trouble understanding the subject in their mother tongue, ChatGPT can translate text into many languages. For this lodging, an illustration of a prompt would be:

Any sentence in English might be used as the input text for "Translate this sentence into Spanish."

5. Specialized instructions

Students with various disabilities may find ChatGPT's ability to generate prompts adapted to each student's abilities and needs useful. For this lodging, an illustration of a prompt would be:

The input text could read, "Generate a conversation about a particular issue, taking into consideration the student's language and cognitive abilities," and the conversation topic or a description of the student's language and cognitive abilities.

As with any tool, the usefulness of ChatGPT depends on how it is used and incorporated into the curriculum. It is advised to use ChatGPT in addition to conventional methods, not as a substitute, to accommodate students with disabilities. To make sure ChatGPT is the right tool for each student's unique needs, you can also provide them comments and direction as they use it and confer with an expert or therapist. The offered prompts are only intended as examples and can be modified to meet the particular needs of the student.

7.5 Peer-to-Peer Learning and Collaboration

Students can learn from one another and develop their talents by working together and helping one another in the classroom. Collaboration and peer assistance can be facilitated in a variety of ways using language models like ChatGPT. Group writing is one possible application for ChatGPT in collaborative settings. A group of students may, for instance, produce a group project using a ChatGPT-powered application, which would then recommend sentences or paragraphs based on the input from each participant. This might be especially helpful for students who need to divide the burden on a group project or who have various writing styles.

Peer review is yet another potential use case. A student could upload a piece of writing to a ChatGPT-powered service, and other students would subsequently provide a critique. This may be particularly useful for students who are unable to receive feedback from a writing tutor or who require more assistance to advance their writing abilities.

A ChatGPT-powered tool can be used by students to practise speaking and writing in a foreign language with other students as part of a third use case for language learning. Students who are learning a new language and require more speaking and writing practice might find this to be extremely beneficial.

Three examples of ChatGPT prompts for group work and peer support:

For our group project, kindly create a statement using ideas from each group member.

"Please have other students comment on this piece of writing's grammar and style."

Please produce a Spanish response to a conversation on the subject of "daily routine"

While ChatGPT might help with cooperation and peer support, it shouldn't take the place of interpersonal contact and interaction.

Chapter Summary

Intelligent tutoring systems (ITS), which employ artificial intelligence and other cutting-edge technology to give students individualised and adaptable learning, were covered in Chapter 7. The chapter focuses on how ChatGPT and other language models can be used to provide students with individualised teaching and content based on their performance and preferences. The chapter also discusses the usage of ChatGPT for adaptive testing, which adapts to the student's level of understanding and offers a more precise evaluation of their abilities. The chapter discusses the advantages of implementing ChatGPT in ITS, including how it can increase student motivation, engagement, and learning outcomes. However, it also stresses that personalization is not a one-size-fits-all solution and should be used in conjunction with other teaching strategies and methods for a more all-encompassing approach to education.

CHAPTER EIGHT

CONSCIOUS USE

The proper use of sophisticated language models, such as ChatGPT, is covered in this chapter, with a focus on minimising the possibility of plagiarism. We must take into account the possibility of plagiarism and make sure that the usage of ChatGPT is consistent with academic integrity as these models grow increasingly common in a variety of industries and fields, including education. In this chapter, we will look at the possibility of plagiarism when utilising ChatGPT and talk about the best ways to prevent it, including citation, transparency, and continual oversight. We will also talk about how to make sure that the academic integrity of the work produced by ChatGPT and other cutting-edge language models for professional and academic development. The chapter will go into detail about plagiarism as well as automation, job displacement, and reskilling for the AI workforce. We must take into account the impact on the workforce as AI continues to upend many industries, and we must look into ways to assist employees in assuming new tasks and developing the skills required to use AI technology. The last section of this chapter offers recommendations for professionals, educators, and students who are preparing to take their place in the AI revolution.

8.1 Reducing the Chance of Plagiarism

A versatile teaching tool and research/productivity help, ChatGPT is a new AI chatbot created by OpenAI that can respond quickly and accurately to a variety of unstructured stimuli. Students, researchers, and professionals can all benefit from this resource since it makes it easier for them to obtain knowledge faster and does tasks more effectively. However, several issues have been brought up regarding the possibility of plagiarism and cheating when using such programmes. Fortunately, we are aware of how to utilise ChatGPT correctly and know when to cite sources to prevent plagiarism-related concerns.

Teachers are concerned because some students are utilising ChatGPT to commit academic fraud by passing off assignments and ideas that they did not create as their own. In response, some schools have blocked access to the tool, but the author claims that this is the incorrect course of action. Instead, schools can use ChatGPT as a customised teaching tool to foster student innovation and prepare them for future employment with AI systems. Because students will discover ways to access ChatGPT outside of the classroom and because AI chatbots may be taught to watermark their outputs to help teachers detect its use, banning ChatGPT from schools won't be effective.

"Yes, a school may restrict access to the ChatGPT website on school computers and networks. However, students can access it outside of class using their phones, laptops, and a variety of other devices. (Just for fun, I spoke with ChatGPT about how a student determined to use the programme may get over a school-wide ban. It offered five solutions, including one that suggested utilising a VPN to mask the student's web usage.) "

As a teacher, one of my main worries is that students can mistakenly believe that ideas they did not come up with are their own when using ChatGPT as a teaching and research tool. This may result in plagiarism problems, which could have detrimental effects on both the particular student and the institution as a whole.

Several steps can be taken to lower the danger of plagiarism when using ChatGPT. Teaching students how to utilise the technology properly, emphasising the value of citing sources when necessary, is one efficient strategy. This can be accomplished through seminars, training sessions, or curriculum inclusion of material on academic honesty and plagiarism.

Utilizing tools that can automatically check student work for instances of plagiarism is another strategy. This can be incorporated into the grading procedure, enabling instructors to find and fix any potential problems right away.

To check for plagiarism, you can also use Turnitin, Grammarly, Plagscan, and other tools.

In an interview with Yahoo Finance Live, Edward Tian discussed his product, GPTZero, a tool that detects the use of ChatGPT technology, as well as the importance of AI in education. By offering a perplexity score and a GPTZero score, GPTZero enables users to copy and paste text to determine whether it was written manually or artificially. GPTZero is not perfect, according to Tian, but over 23,000 instructors have joined the product's wait list for its professional use. Additionally, he says that he aims to responsibly deploy this technology and to have the tools and protections necessary to prevent its exploitation.

Encourage students to use ChatGPT independently and critically to further limit the likelihood of plagiarism. This can be achieved by giving students prompts that demand them to do more than just repeat information from the tool; they must also analyse, understand, and evaluate it. Last but not least, institutions need to have explicit policies and processes in place for dealing with plagiarism, as well as measures to make sure that students are aware of these policies and the potential repercussions of breaking them. This may result in penalties like failing the assignment, failing the course, or, in extreme circumstances, expulsion. We may take precautions to lessen the possibility of plagiarism and make sure that students are using ChatGPT properly and ethically. ChatGPT can be a useful teaching and research tool.

8.2 Appropriate Credit

When using ChatGPT or any other language model, proper attribution is essential. We must provide due credit to the model's designers and mention the information's original recommended practisespracticesng ChatGPT and other language models in various situations, such as in research papers, presentations, and online content, which will be covered in this area. This will include recommendations for citing the model, including links to the source code and documentation, and revealing any model adjustments or pre-processing. We can make sure that the efforts of those who developed ChatGPT and other language models are acknowledged and valued by adhering to these rules.

In a recent examination of submission guidelines for studies utilising ChatGPT, Nature discovered:

1. Nature's editor-in-chief in London, Magdalena Skipper, asserts that LLMs cannot be successfully held accountable for their work when authorship is acknowledged.

2. Holden Thorp, the executive editor of the Washin, DC-based Science family of journals, adds, "We would not allow AI to be identified as an author on a paper we published, and use of AI-generated content without proper citation may be considered plagiarism."

3. According to Sabina Alam, Director of Publishing Ethics and Integrity at Taylor & Francis in London, authors are accountable for the truthfulness of their work and should make any use of LLMs clear in the acknowledgements section or an equivalent.

A sharing and publication policy has been established by OpenAI for ChatGPT, their AI-generated material. As long as the content is credited to the user's name or business and makes it abundantly obvious that it was generated using AI, the policy permits posting and sharing prompts and completions on social media, and livestrealive streaming demonstrations to groups of people. Additionally, it forbids the dissemination of material that offends others or is in violation of OpenAI's content policy. First-party written content co-authored with the OpenAI API must be ascribed to the user, the AI's contribution to the content must be explicitly revealed, and the content must adhere to OpenAI's content policy or terms to publish it. The research policy welcomes research articles pertaininaboutAI API and permits the evaluation of their work and products by a wider audience.

OpenAI provided the following language as a forward/introduction/equivalent suggestion:

> This text was created in part using OpenAI's large-scale language-generation model GPT-3. The author, who is ultimately responsible for this publication's content, reviewed, edited, and amended the wording after it had been generated as a draught.

The significance of declaring the use of ChatGPT when speaking with others has been covered by reputable research outlets. They have underlined that to confidence and prevent confusion, we must be open about the usage of AI-generated solutions. Some have recommended including a disclaimer in email signatures or making the message's source known. The difficulty of distinguishing between responses generated by humans and artificial intelligence (AI) may get harder as technology advances, according to some academics, which emphasises the significance of proper disclosure. In general, research sources have underlined the importance of honesty and transparency when using ChatGPT for any kind of communication.

8.3 Workforce Retraining and Displacement

As automation and machine learning develop, developing concern is that AI will replace human workers. Workers in some industries may lose their jobs as more duties are taken over by automated systems and AI. Retraining and upskilling, however, can lessen this problem. Utilizing conversational AI bots like ChatGPT and other tools of a like nature is one approach to do this. These systems can give employees the chance to pick up new skills and adjust to the shifting nature of the labour market. They can also be utilised to improve human workers‘ talents, enabling them to collaborate with machines and AI systems in complimencomplementaryis can result in workflows that are more effective and productive while also ensuring that employees are still in demand in the face of rapid technology advancement.

Responsible users of conversational AI solutions like ChatGPT can gain enormous advantages for their businesses as well as for any employees whose jobs may be affected by automation. Using these technologies to retrain and upgrade employees' skills is a crucial opportunity. Workers can acquire new skills and change with the job market by having access to a conversational AI agent like ChatGPT, for instance. This can involve picking up new technical skills in disciplines like data science and machine learning as well as learning how to communicate with and manage AI systems.

Another chance for responsible adopters is to employ conversational AI tools to enhance rather than replace the skills of human workers. Workflows can be automated using ChatGPT and other similar systems, freeing up human employees to concentrate on more difficult and innovative activities. This can result in workflows that are more effective and productive while also ensuring that employees are still in demand in the face of rapid technologtechnologicalent.

Additionally, conscientious adopters can leverage ChatGPT and other conversational AI solutions to enhance customer engagement and service. Organizations may enhance the customer experience, forge closer bonds with their consumers, and boost customer satisfaction and loyalty—all of which will result in higher sales and revenue.

In conclusion, thoughtful users of conversational AI technologies like ChatGPT have the chance to raise the effectiveness and performance of their businesses while also making an aninvestinguture of their workforce. They may contribute to ensuring that everyone enjoys the advantages of automation by using these tools responsibly.

8.3.1 Adopting ChatGPT responsibly with students

Use ChatGPT appropriately in the context of your course, university, field, and society as a student. Consider:

1. Recognize ChatGPT's potential and constraints.

Although ChatGPT is an effective tool for text generation, it is not perfect and occasionally produces biased obiasedropriate language. Be aware of these restrictions and handle the tool with care.

"Explain the ChatGPT model's text generation capabilities and constraints."

2. Give due credit to the source

Be careful to properly credit the author if you use ChatGPT in your academic work or study by citing the model and include including the source code and documentation.

“Give an illustration of how to properly credit sources when utilising the ChatGPT model in a research article.”

3. Be open and honest about adjusting.

In your work, be honest about any pre-processing or fine-tuning that was carried out if you modified the model to suit a particular purpose or area.

Explain how the ChatGPT model is adjusted for a particular assignment and why it's critical to be open and honest about it in your work.

4. Recognize the rules of your university.

As you utilise ChatGPT, be sure to adhere to your university's restrictions on the use of AI in coursework and research.

"Recap the policies at your university for employing AI in coursework and research."

5. Apply it morally

Put into reality the ethical issues surrounding AI, such as accountability, justice, privacy, and academic integrity.

"In terms of academic integrity, privacy, fairness, and responsibility describe how to apply the ChatGPT paradigm in an esthetically

6. Employ it as a tool

A tool is ChatGPT. It can be used to promote and enhance critical thinking and creativity, but it is not a replacement for them.

"Give an illustration of how ChatGPT might be applied as a tool to foster creativity and critical thinking in a particular business or profession."

7. Examine the output that the model produced.

Always check the accuracy and applicability of the output produced by the ChatGPT model to your assignment. The output of the model should not be relied upon without further examination and analysis.

"Explain how to evaluate the ChatGPT model's output for a particular task and why it's necessary to do critical review and analysis before relying exclusively on the model's output."

8. Check for plagiarism

Use a plagiarism detector to make sure any work produced by ChatGPT is original and free of plagiarism before submitting it as your own. By doing this, you can prevent yourself from unintentionally engaging in academic dishonesty.

"Give an example of a plagiarism detection programme and discuss the value of utilising one before submitting work created with ChatGPT."

Recognize the ChatGPT model's training data constraints and take action to resolve them when utilising the model. This can entail using a variety of representative training data or applying debiasing techniques to lessen the effect of biases on the model's output.

Furthermore, it is advised to think about the social effects of AI use, including ChatGPT, as well as any potential effects on job displacement and other societal issues. Find out more about these consequences, and think about how to reduce any potential drawbacks from using them.

As a student, it is imperative to use ChatGPT responsibly by being aware of its strengths and weaknesses, properly attributing sources, being open about fine-tuning, being aware of university policies, using it ethically, using it as a tool, evaluating the output produced by the model, being aware of potential biases and inaccuracies in the training data, and taking into account the potential effects of AI use on society.

8.3.2 Appropriate ChatGPT Use by Teachers

Many teachers are using ChatGPT to facilitate discussions, generate ideas, and complete writing projects as the usage of AI technology in the classroom increases. But like with any new technology, there are concerns regarding responsible usage.

Many of my colleagues are wondering, "What should I say about ChatGPT in my syllabus?" in anticipation of the numerous potential use cases for ChatGPT.

There are three potential ChatGPT policy positions:

1. "ChatGPT usage is not permitted for any assignments or in-class activities. The student must have finished and submitted all of the work. Academic consequences will ensue from using ChatGPT in this class.

2. "ChatGPT may be used as a tool for homework and class projects, but all material presented must be original and reference any text produced by the model. It is entirely forbidden to turn in work for class without acknowledging that a model was used, and failing to do so will result in academic consequences.

3. Co-writing with ChatGPT is presumptive. Students in this course are free to use ChatGPT as they see fit and are not required to reveal it.

Leading the class in appropriate stewardship of new technology in the classroom, within the context of your courses, university, field, and society is the educator's role. When using ChatGPT for outreach, research, and teaching, there are several factors to take into account. When integrating ChatGPT into your curriculum, take into account:

1. The course's setting

• When using ChatGPT in the classroom, educators need to set clear expectations for students and give them cleat ructions.

• Educators should make sure that using ChatGPT supports the course's learning objectives and improves student engagement and learning.

• Teachers should instruct and guide students on how to utilise ChatGPT ethically and with proper credit, among other things.

2. The academic setting

• Academics should be aware of and abide by the university's rules and regulations regarding the use of AI in the classroom and research

• Teachers must make sure that ChatGPT use is consistent with the goals and principles of the school.

• Be open about utilising ChatGPT in their research and instruction, and offer chances for student and colleague feedback and input.

3. The environment

• Gain knowledge of the most recent advancements in AI research and application, such as ChatGPT.

• Educators should follow industry standards for ethical behaviour and think about the ethical implications of using ChatGPT in research and scholarship.

• Provide chances for peer and community feedback and input, and be open about using ChatGPT in research and scholarship.

4. The social environment

• When using ChatGPT, educators should think about how it will affect society as a whole, taking into account concerns about accountability, fairness, and privacy.

• Teachers need to make sure that using ChatGPT is consistent with society's issues.

• Teachers should give students the chance to interact and converse with the larger community about using ChatGPT responsibly.

When using ChatGPT responsibly for your teaching, research, and outreach activities as an educator, there are several rings to take into account. Here are some crucial areas to concentrate on:

1. Academic Honesty

It's crucial to make sure that students aren't cheating or plagiarising when utilising ChatGPT in the classroom. Incorporating plagiarism detection technologies, outlining your expectations for applying the model in assignments, and offering advice on proper credit are a few examples of how to do this.

2. Data Security and Privacy

It's crucial to make sure that any data used to train or improve the model is appropriately safeguarded and protected while utilising ChatGPT in your research. This may entail gaining participants' informed consent, removing any personally identifiable information from data, and making sure that all data storage and sharing adhere to tadheretutional and legal requirements.

3. Moral Points of View

Think about the model's ethical implications before employing ChatGPT in your outreach, research, or teaching. This may involve concerns with justice, accountability, and issues of bias.

4. Accessibility

It's crucial to make sure the ChatGPT model is accessible to all students, regardless of their backgrounds or skills, when using it in teaching, research, or outreach. This can entail offering different forms, like audio or video, or giving students with disabilities more support and accommodations.

5. Transparency

It's critical to be open and honest about the model's capabilities and constraints, as well as any pre-processing or tuning that has been done when utilising ChatGPT for teaching, research, or outreach. This may entail explaining this knowledge to students or research participants in a straightforward manner and giving documentation on the model's application.

6. Institutional Guidelines

It's crucial to be aware of and adhere to any institutional AI usage regulations while utilising ChatGPT for teaching, research, or outreach. This could include policies on data privacy, academic honesty, or moral conduct in research.

7. Professional Growth

Educators can take advantage of professional development opportunities to stay up to date on the most recent findings and industry best practises practices to ensure the appropriate te use of ChatGPT. Prudent workers will recognise and pursue training to expand their AI skill set to prosper in the modern economy as the workforce becomes more automated with AI-informed processes.

8. Collaboration

Working together with other educators, researchers, and subject-matter experts can be a fantastic way to learn about the most recent innovations, ethical issues, and best practisespracticesng for the use of ChatGPT in outreach, teaching, and research.

University educators can use ChatGPT ethically and responsibly in their teaching, research, and outreach efforts by taking into account these contexts and best practises practices

8.3.3 Professionals should use ChatGPT responsibly

Regarding the ethical usage of ChatGPT when communicating with clients, coworkers, colleagues, professional associations, and people in your field:

1. Be open and honest about how you utilise technology. Inform your clients, coworkers, and industry associations of your use of a language model like ChatGPT and any technical constraints.

2. ChatGPT may have biases because it was trained on such a large amount of Internet content. Be mindful of bias when utilising the techno and make an effort to avoid it.

3. Enhance rather than replace human relationships with technology. Although ChatGPT might be a useful tool for automating routine chores or quickly presenting information, it shouldn't be utilised for human interactions.

4. Honor the security and privacy of your coworkers and clients. Ensure that you adhere to all laws and rules governing data security and privacy.

5. Remain current with the most recent innovations and industry best practisespracticesbout the most recent technological advancements and the best ways to use language models like ChatGPT.

In conclusion, the ethical uthe usage of ChatGPT necessitates openness, understanding of potential biases, balancing with human interactions, considerations for privacy and security, and ongoing learning.

CHAPTER NINE

CONCLUSION

9.1 Students Next Step

Large-scale language model ChatGPT, created by OpenAI, may transform industries. Using ChatGPT to create a new project or business can be a fantastic opportunity for students or entrepreneurs. But it's crucial to comprehend the technology's potential and constraints as well as the moral issues raised by its application.

Setting up ChatGPT requires you to first establish your aims and objectives in detail. Know what you want ChatGPT to do for you and how it ties into your larger project or business plan. You can begin experimenting with various uses for ChatGPT after you have a solid idea of what it is capable of.

Natural language processing is one of ChatGPT's most promising uses. With the aid of this technology, repetitive operations, including promptly responding to consumer inquiries or giving information, can be automated. Additionally, ChatGPT's language translation features can be applied to open up new client and market opportunities. ChatGPT can also be used to generate text, which can be utilised to produce fresh material like news articles or product descriptions.

It's crucial to obtain input and iterate as you test out various ChatGPT applications. Get feedback on your solution and test your concepts on actual users. Utilize this criticism to refine and enhance your answer. A competent team with a diversified range of abilities is necessary to build a successful project or business. When assembling your team, search for individuals that can enhance your talents and contribute fresh viewpoints.

It's also crucial to educate yourself on current trends and the best ways to use language models like ChatGPT.

Learn about the most recent technological advancements and the best ways to use language models like ChatGPT. You can stay ahead of the curve and enhance your solution by continuing to study.

Finally, it's critical to comprehend the ethical ramifications of using ChatGPT. Being an AI model, ChatGPT has ethical ramifications that must be taken into account, including biases, data privacy, and security. Ensure that you abide by all laws and regulations and that the ethical principles guiding the use of the model are obvious to you. Students and businesspeople can use ChatGPT to create inventive ideas and advertise them by following these guidelines.

9.2 Educators Next Step

The newest technological advancements and how they might be applied to improve student learning must be known by educators. One such innovation is ChatGPT, a sizable language model created by OpenAI that has the potential to fundamentally change how we educate people.

Teachers need to comprehend ChatGPT's capabilities and constraints before they can use it effectively in their lessons. This entails giving them the instruction and tools they need to use the technology in their classroom efficiently. In order to keep up with the most recent advancements in the area, educators should be urged to collaborate, share their experiences, and best practises.

Including ChatGPT in pertinent courses like computer science, artificial intelligence, or natural language processing is crucial. As a result, our kids will have the chance to interact with and learn about technology in a meaningful way. Additionally, we must routinely assess the efficiency of using ChatGPT in the classroom. Analyzing student engagement and comprehension as well as the overall effect on student learning are included in this.

Additionally, it's critical to motivate students to keep investigating ChatGPT's potential in independent projects, academic work, and professional settings. They will be able to keep up with industry advancements and get ready for professions in related industries in the future thanks to this.

Finally, it's critical to comprehend the ethical ramifications of using ChatGPT. We must take into account ChatGPT's ethical implications for use, including biases, data privacy, and security, because it is an AI model. Ensure that you abide by all laws and regulations and that the ethical principles guiding the use of the model are obvious to you.

Universities can successfully integrate ChatGPT into their curricula and better educate students for the future by following these actions. To make sure that our kids are receiving the greatest education possible, it is crucial to consistently learn about new advancements and best practises in using language models like ChatGPT.

9.3 Professionals' Next Step

As a professional, adding ChatGPT to your workflow can be an effective way to boost productivity and simplify work. But it's crucial to use it with a strategy in place and a set of objectives in mind. To advance your professional development with ChatGPT, consider these actions when utilising it for work-related tasks:

1. Experiment in novel and creative ways with the model. You could, for instance, use ChatGPT to generate dialogue for a chatbot or virtual assistant or to generate creative writing, such short stories or poems.
2. Examine the potential ChatGPT applications in sectors that have not before been studied. You may, for instance, look at how the model might increase the effectiveness of financial analysis or medical research.
3. Disseminate your research and experiences to colleagues in your field via publications, blog postings, or talks at conferences. This will help your research get out there and will also give you the chance to seek comments from other experts in the field.
4. Work diligently to enhance the model's performance by honing it on certain tasks or data sets and experimenting with various training strategies.
5. To assist others in learning about and using ChatGPT, think about coaching others or developing teaching materials. For instance, you could write tutorials or sample code to assist others in getting started, or you could organise seminars to impart the fundamentals of using language models.

By doing these things, you'll stay on the cutting edge of your industry and contribute significantly to the creation and use of ChatGPT.

9.4 Final Phrases

In conclusion, ChatGPT is a flexible tool for writing, learning, and creating material, with a wide range of uses in higher education and other fields. We must utilise it in an ethical and responsible manner and take precautions to prevent plagiarism. In order to improve our critical thinking and inventiveness as students and businesspeople, we must be aware of the technology's advantages and disadvantages. As instructors, we may meaningfully integrate ChatGPT into our curriculum and celebrate the most recent technological advancements. As we train the next generation of leaders for the AI-powered workforce, we can be sure that we are using ChatGPT in a responsible and ethical manner by adhering to these guidelines.

The huge language model called ChatGPT, created by OpenAI, is a potent tool with many possible uses. However, there are issues with its utilisation, such as the possibility of plagiarism and cheating. Schools and institutions must adopt ChatGPT as a teaching tool and create measures for lowering the possibility of plagiarism in order to allay these worries. This can be done by instructing students on how to use the tool properly, utilising plagiarism detection software, and putting in place clear standards for dealing with plagiarism. When employing ChatGPT in any setting, including research papers, presentations, and online content, it's also crucial to maintain accurate attribution and transparency. Additionally, educators and students should be prepared for the social consequences of AI use, including ChatGPT, as well as any potential effects on job displacement and other social issues. Students and teachers who want to use ChatGPT responsibly need to be aware of its strengths and weaknesses, work together to share best practises, integrate it into courses that are relevant to it, regularly evaluate how well it is being used, and keep looking into its applications in projects, research, and business.

9 798889 752240

Printed by Libri Plureos GmbH in Hamburg,
Germany